# Father

# A BOOK FOR MY FATHER

## WELLERAN POLTARNEES

LAUGHING ELEPHANT         MMIII

ISBN 1-883211-65-4

FIRST PRINTING   ALL RIGHTS RESERVED   PRINTED IN CHINA

LAUGHING ELEPHANT BOOKS
3645 INTERLAKE AVENUE NORTH   SEATTLE, WA   98103


WWW.LAUGHINGELEPHANT.COM

# Dear Father:

I lovingly offer you
this book in thanks
for your many
contributions to my life.

*All my Love,*
*Wicki*

I am grateful for the work
you did for your family,
the support you offered
when we most needed it.

Thanks for your strong work ethic,
it has been the reason I can
able to support my family today.

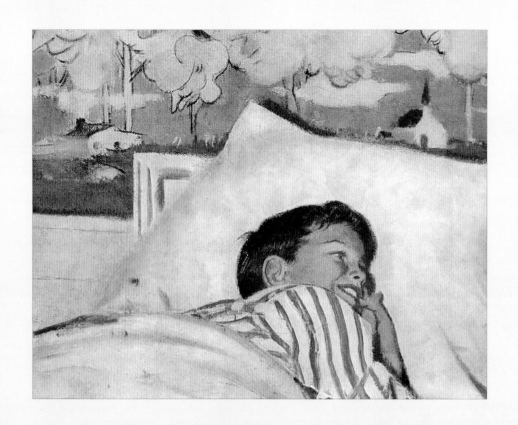

You gave us
enriching memories
of your boyhood,

Stories about your dog, Teenie,
and you and Uncle Charlie playing
pool at Ohio State (and not going to class).

and told stories which
I will always remember.

The one about you and Uncle Charlie
painting grandma's front porch and
her getting mad because you all
balanced the furniture on the wall
of the porch. I was thinking about that
story yesterday when I was cleaning
my front porch.

You were strong when
we needed your strength,

*I still think youru Strength offers
me Safety and Security.*

and gentler when
gentleness was needed.

*your gentleness was hidden
behind your humor and still is
but when it's not I know it
comes from your heart (and even
when it is from humor I know it
comes from your heart just not as deep)*

Many of your enthusiasms
became mine,
for you held them
so wisely and keenly.

*Your enthusiasm for golf has enriched my boys lives.*

Your skills were many,

I always thought you could fix anything.

and your
practical wisdom bountiful.

*Thanks for all your wisdom through
my divorce. I couldn't have gotten
through it without you.*

When I was little,
you made me feel
well taken care of.

I remember when we were at the
Washington Monument and I was
afraid to walk down the steps - you
stayed with me the whole way down.

You helped teach me
the deep satisfactions of play,

I loved when you would
wrestle with us on the
floor. Why did I think I
might win?

and the joy of laughter.

*Thanks for my sense on humor!*

I am grateful that
you listened
to my young ideas.

I remember when I didn't get in the
high school sorority I wanted and was
crying in the bathroom on Lanesboro. You
comforted me and made me feel less
rejected.

25

You dreamed a future for me,
helping me realize my own.

I remember driving down LaGrange Rd.
with you and having a conversation
about college majors. I didn't follow your
advice, of course, but that conversation
always made me know I could do anything
I put my mind to.

Whenever I wandered,
I always knew
you believed in my destiny.

Thanks for your support through
life's difficulties.

I am mindful of
your many generous acts.

To name just a few:
- coming to louisville when I
  needed you here
- sending me to college
- many memorable vacations

I send you my gratitude
and love.

# Colophon

Designed at Blue Lantern Studio
by Mike Harrison and Sacheverell Darling

Typeset in Bembo

# Picture Credits